Picture Reference

EARTH

BARBARA TAYLOR

How to use this book

Contents
The contents page at the front of this book lists the main subjects in the book and the pages on which you can find them.

Cross-references
Above the heading on the page, you will find a list of subjects that are related to the topic. These subjects are listed with their page numbers. Turn to these pages to find out more about each subject.

Glossary words
Difficult words are explained in the glossary on page 46. These words are written in **bold**. Look them up in the glossary to find out what they mean.

Index
The index is on pages 47–48. It is a list of important words mentioned in the book in alphabetical order, with the page numbers written next to them. If you want to read about a subject, look it up in the index, then turn to the page number given.

Titles in this series
Animals
Atlas
Earth
Space
Transport

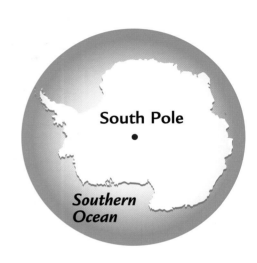

Created and published by
Two-Can Publishing Ltd
346 Old Street
London
EC1V 9NQ

Senior designer: Helen McDonagh
Senior commissioning editor: Jacqueline McCann
Art director: Belinda Webster
Managing editor: Deborah Kespert
Editorial assistant: Lucy Arnold
Consultant: Carmela Di Landro
Main illustrations: Brian McIntyre
Computer illustrations: Mel Pickering, Jacqueline Land
Large computer illustrations p4-5, p6: Sebastian Quigley
Picture research: Laura Cartwright
Production: Leila Peerun

Hardback ISBN 1-85434-601-6
Paperback ISBN 1-85434-617-2

Dewey Decimal Classification 550

Hardback 2 4 6 8 10 9 7 5 3 1
Paperback 2 4 6 8 10 9 7 5 3 1

A catalogue record for this book is available from the British Library.

Photographic credits:
Bruce Coleman Ltd/Jeff Foot Productions p14b, BCL/Keith Gunner p15br, BCL/John Shaw p26, BCL/Michael Fogden p35t, BCL/Andrew Purcell p35b, BCL p37t, BCL/George McCarthy p39t; NHPA p14tl, NHPA/Gerard Lacz p34b; Oxford Scientific Films/Warren Faidley p37b; Pictor International p21b; Planet Earth Pictures/I & V Krafft/Hoa Qui p7t, PEP p13, PEP/Adam Jones p17t; Robert Harding Picture Library/Michio Hoshino p34t, RHPL/JHC Wilson p39b; Science Photo Library/Simon Fraser p9t, p40, SPL/Sinclair Stammers p15t, SPL/NOAA p41tl, SPL/Marcelo Brodsky p41b; Telegraph Colour Library p41tr; The National Geographic Society/David S Boyer p29; The Stock Market p7b; Tony Stone Images/Chris Noble p8, TSI/James Balog p9b, TSI/AB Wadham p14tr, TSI/John Callahan p17b, TSI/Greg Probst p22, TSI p23, TSI/James Strachan p25t, TSI/Andy Sacks p25b, TSI/Gary Yeowell p36; Zefa/Spichtinger p21t.

Printed and bound in Spain by Graficas Reunidas

Contents

How the Earth began

The Earth is the name of the **planet** where we live. It is a huge ball of rock spinning through space. No one is sure when the Earth began, but some scientists think that, between 10 and 20 **billion** years ago, there was a huge explosion, called the **Big Bang**. Gradually, over millions of years, stars and planets started to form. One of these planets was Earth.

▼ Some scientists believe that, about 4.5 billion years ago, the Earth formed in this way.

2 Over millions of years, grains of dust and ice in the clouds stuck together to make bigger and bigger pieces.

1 The Earth may have started as clouds of **gas** and dust swirling round the Sun.

▼ How life began

Life on Earth probably started in the oceans between 3 and 4 billion years ago. At first, there were only plants and simple living creatures called bacteria. Later, animals without backbones appeared, then, animals with backbones. Gradually, life moved from the ocean on to the land.

Over 1,000 million years ago, animals with soft bodies, such as jellyfish and worms, developed in the sea. They were the first living things.

By 500 million years ago, fish had appeared. Then, 370 million years ago, fish-like creatures that breathed air moved from the ocean on to the land.

3 Slowly, an enormous round ball of hot, fiery rock formed. The Earth was surrounded by a layer of gases.

4 Eventually, the surface cooled and formed a hard, rocky **crust**. Drops of water in the air made clouds. Rain fell into dips on the surface of the Earth to make oceans.

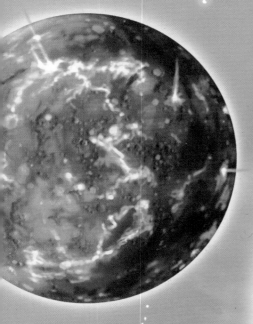

Around 240 million years ago, dinosaurs roamed the Earth. Other **reptiles**, such as crocodiles and turtles, also developed around this time.

Large **mammals** and birds appeared on Earth about 140 million years ago. Together, they took the place of the dinosaurs.

Humans may have first walked on the Earth 2 million years ago. These people made the first tools. Humans like us have been around for only about 40,000 years.

Go to How the Earth began page 4, Rock and fossil page 14, Volcano page 12

Inside the Earth

Planet Earth is a ball of rock and metal, made up of four layers. The thin, cool, outside layer is called the **crust**. People live on the surface of the crust. The three layers inside the Earth are thicker and much hotter than the crust. No one knows exactly what the Earth is like inside, but we do know that the hottest part is in the middle.

land and ocean
Most of the crust is covered by ocean, but other parts are dry land with soil on top.

Layers of the Earth
This picture shows the layers that make up the Earth. The thickest layer lies just under the crust and is called the **mantle**. Below the mantle, there is an outer and an inner core.

Earth's crust
The thin crust is made of solid rock. It forms a skin, like the skin of an apple, around the planet.

mantle
This is a thick layer of rock. Rock close to the crust is melted and flows up and down, inside the Earth.

inner core
The centre of the planet is a ball of solid metal that may be as hot as 7,000°C.

outer core
Outside the solid inner core, there is a layer of liquid metals that is fiercely hot.

Rocks inside the Earth

Melted rock that flows in the Earth's mantle is called **magma**. Sometimes, magma pushes its way up through a crack in the Earth's crust, called a **volcano**. Then, it flows along the ground like a hot, red river. When magma reaches the surface, it is called **lava**.

Soil on the surface

Soil is made up of tiny pieces of rock from the Earth's crust. It also contains plant and animal remains that make the soil rich and help plants to grow.

tunnels
Worm burrows let air and water into the soil.

roots
Plant roots help to hold the soil together.

bedrock
Beneath the soil lies the solid rock of the Earth's crust. This is called bedrock.

Mining the Earth

Deep within the crust, there are fuels such as **oil** and **gas**. They formed millions of years ago from rotted plants and animals. Today, miners drill down to 5,000 metres to find oil and gas trapped between layers of rock. Then the fuel is used to make electricity in power stations.

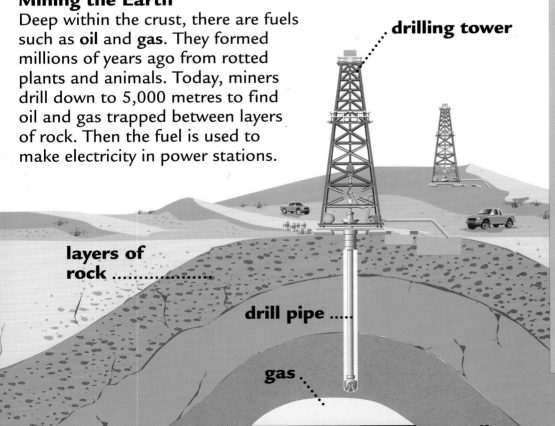

drilling tower

layers of rock

drill pipe

gas

oil

Quarries

At the surface, miners dig large pits called quarries. Rocks are broken up by huge machines and used for building. Metals are taken from the rocks to make machinery.

Go to Earthquake page 10, Mountain page 30, Ocean page 18, Where on Earth? page 42

Continent

A **continent** is a huge area of land. There are seven continents on the Earth. Each continent sits on top of a giant piece of the Earth's **crust** called a **plate**. There are 19 large plates and a few smaller ones. Every year, the plates move a few centimetres. Over millions of years, these movements make the oceans and continents shift and change shape.

▶ This map shows the seven continents and some of the Earth's plates that lie beneath them.

Plates

The Earth's plates fit together like a jigsaw puzzle. Plates float on top of the Earth's **mantle**, like rafts on the sea. Some plates have ocean on top, others have a continent, or part of a continent, as well as ocean.

African Plate

This plate is called the African Plate. It includes the part of the Earth's crust under the continent of Africa and some crust under the ocean.

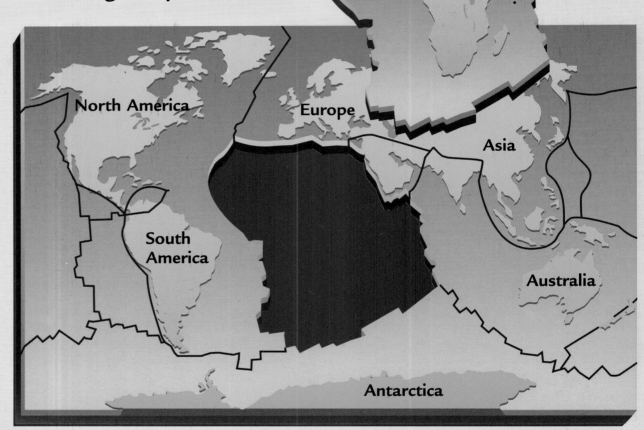

Plates pushing together

When two of the Earth's plates crash into each other, the crust at the edge of the plates crumples and folds. Over millions of years, the crust is gradually pushed upwards into high mountain peaks. This is how the Himalayan Mountains were formed. The Himalayas are the world's highest mountains. They are still growing taller because the plates are still pushing together.

Plates pulling apart

On some parts of the Earth's crust, huge plates pull apart. This happens mostly under the ocean, but sometimes plates pull away from each other under the land. Iceland is a country that sits on two plates that are pulling apart. This has made a long, deep crack in the land, as shown in the photograph. Eventually, Iceland will split in two along this crack, but this will not happen for millions of years.

Sliding plates

On other parts of the Earth's crust, plates slide past each other and move slowly in opposite directions. This can make a deep crack in the land. This photograph shows the San Andreas **Fault** in the USA. Two of the Earth's sliding plates meet here and earthquakes often happen.

Continents in the past

Scientists think that about 200 million years ago, all the Earth's land fitted together in one big piece. This was a supercontinent called Pangaea. As the plates moved, they slowly pulled Pangaea apart, making new, smaller continents.

Pangaea 200 million years ago

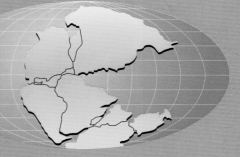

Continents 120 million years ago

Continents today

Earthquake

An earthquake happens when there are sudden movements in the Earth's **crust** that make the ground shake. Most earthquakes are small and we don't notice them, but during large earthquakes, rocks tremble. The land may split apart along a crack in the crust called a **fault line**. Some large fault lines lie above places where the Earth's **plates** meet.

▶ A large earthquake can destroy a city and change the landscape.

3 Fires break out because **gas** pipes and electrical wires are damaged. When water pipes burst, it is difficult for firefighters to put out fires.

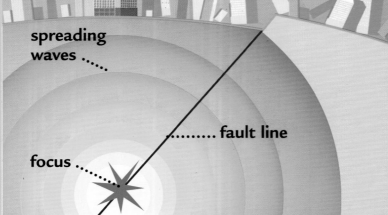

2 Windows break and walls crack. People find it difficult to stay standing.

1 An earthquake starts deep underground but it makes rocks on the surface crack open.

How earthquakes happen
An earthquake starts at a point called the focus. Shock waves spread out from the focus in all directions and eventually reach the surface. Rocks slip past each other and the ground splits open. The waves continue to spread and may do a lot of damage.

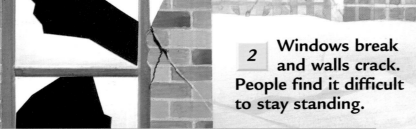

spreading waves ......

.... fault line

focus ......

10

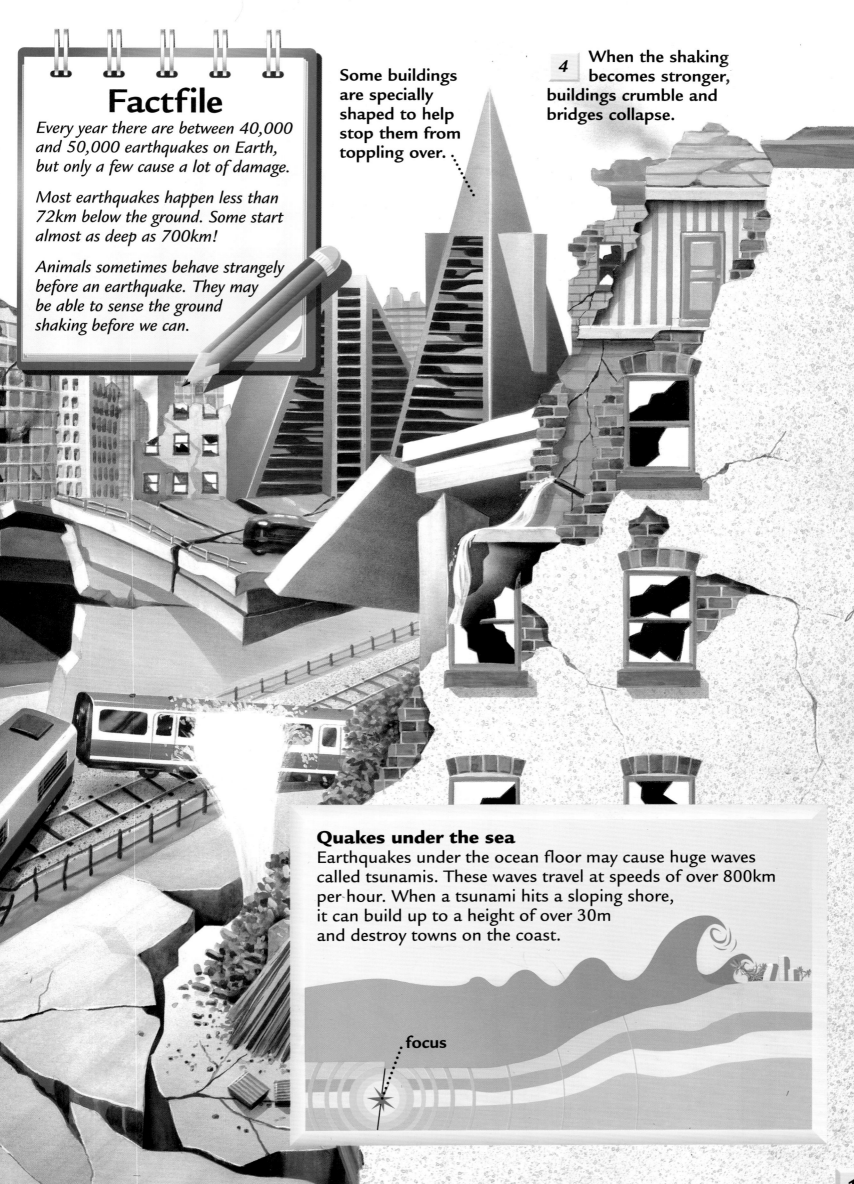

Factfile

Every year there are between 40,000 and 50,000 earthquakes on Earth, but only a few cause a lot of damage.

Most earthquakes happen less than 72km below the ground. Some start almost as deep as 700km!

Animals sometimes behave strangely before an earthquake. They may be able to sense the ground shaking before we can.

Some buildings are specially shaped to help stop them from toppling over.

4 When the shaking becomes stronger, buildings crumble and bridges collapse.

Quakes under the sea

Earthquakes under the ocean floor may cause huge waves called tsunamis. These waves travel at speeds of over 800km per hour. When a tsunami hits a sloping shore, it can build up to a height of over 30m and destroy towns on the coast.

focus

Go to Inside the Earth page 6, Mountain page 30

Volcano

A **volcano** is a crack in the Earth's **crust** through which **gases** and hot, molten rock pour out. Deep underground, in the Earth's **mantle**, there is liquid rock, called **magma**. Sometimes the magma rises up through the Earth's crust and explodes into the air through a crack on the surface. This is called a volcanic eruption.

▶ Most volcanoes erupt through cone-shaped mountains such as this.

The life of a volcano

A volcano that erupts regularly is called 'active'. When a volcano is quiet for many years, we say it is 'dormant', or 'asleep'. Volcanoes that are unlikely to erupt again are called 'extinct'.

Inside a volcano

Magma collects in an underground pool called a magma chamber. Gases in the magma force it to rise up through the crust, making chimneys called vents. Then magma explodes through the top of the volcano and becomes **lava**.

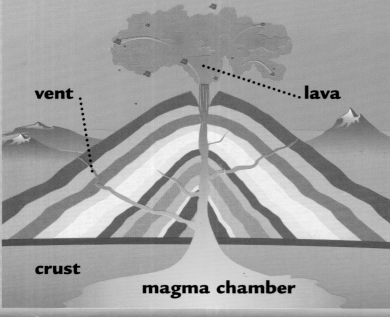

crater

1 Magma bursts through the top of the volcano, leaving behind a hole called a crater.

2 The volcano throws magma, ash and steam high into the air.

Studying volcanoes

People who study volcanoes are called vulcanologists. Often, they wear special suits to protect themselves from lava. Vulcanologists record the temperature of lava and collect samples of gas and rock. This tells them more about rocks that come from inside the Earth.

3 When magma reaches the surface, we call it lava. It flows down the side of the volcano.

lava

Factfile

The word 'volcano' comes from Vulcan, the name of an ancient god of fire.

The highest active volcano is Ojos del Salado, on the border between Chile and Argentina. It is 6,887m high.

Lava can be twelve times hotter than boiling water.

The Hawaiian Islands are the tops of undersea volcanoes.

4 Lava cools and hardens into volcanic rock. Over many years the rock breaks down, forming rich soil that is good for farming.

Go to Erosion page 16, Inside the Earth page 6, Volcano page 12

Rock and fossil

Rock is the solid part of the Earth's surface and forms the Earth's **crust**. Under the ocean, rock is covered by water, but on land rock is often covered with soil. Sometimes, in deserts and on mountains, rock is bare. Rock may be hard or soft. Many interesting things are found inside it, from rare jewels to the remains of ancient animals.

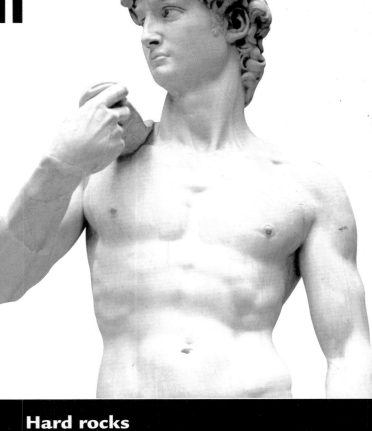

Minerals
All rocks are mixtures of tiny grains called minerals. Some minerals are soft and light, others are hard and dark. Gold and iron are types of minerals, called metals, that are found in rocks. Diamonds, and the opal shown in the photograph, are rare minerals, called gems.

Hard rocks
Marble is a rock that comes in many colours. It can be white, black, red, green, or striped. Marble is one of the world's finest kinds of rock, so it is often polished and used on the fronts of buildings. It is also a hard rock and cannot easily be worn away. For thousands of years, sculptors have carved statues from marble by carefully chiselling the rock.

Soft rocks
The Grand Canyon in the USA is made up of many layers of rock that have been worn away by water. One of the main kinds of rock in the canyon is sandstone, which is made of sand and other pieces of rock. Sandstone is a soft rock. It can be cut and shaped easily, so it is often used for building.

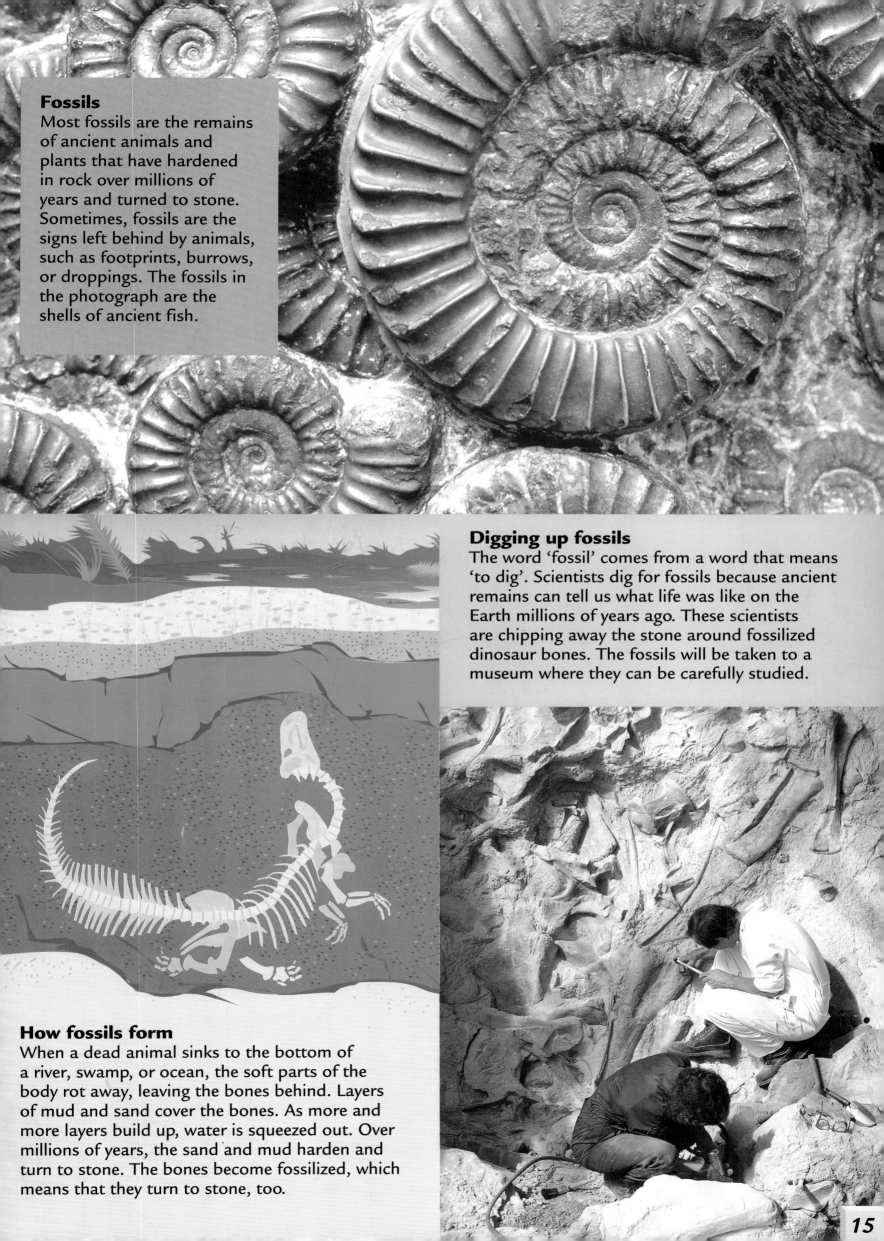

Fossils

Most fossils are the remains of ancient animals and plants that have hardened in rock over millions of years and turned to stone. Sometimes, fossils are the signs left behind by animals, such as footprints, burrows, or droppings. The fossils in the photograph are the shells of ancient fish.

Digging up fossils

The word 'fossil' comes from a word that means 'to dig'. Scientists dig for fossils because ancient remains can tell us what life was like on the Earth millions of years ago. These scientists are chipping away the stone around fossilized dinosaur bones. The fossils will be taken to a museum where they can be carefully studied.

How fossils form

When a dead animal sinks to the bottom of a river, swamp, or ocean, the soft parts of the body rot away, leaving the bones behind. Layers of mud and sand cover the bones. As more and more layers build up, water is squeezed out. Over millions of years, the sand and mud harden and turn to stone. The bones become fossilized, which means that they turn to stone, too.

Go to Desert page 20, Mountain page 30, Ocean page 18, River page 28, Where on Earth? page 42

Erosion

The surface of the Earth is always changing. Oceans, rivers, ice and the wind wear away the land by loosening rocks and breaking them up. Gradually, the rocks are broken into pieces that are small enough to be carried away. This is called **erosion**.

Wave erosion

As the ocean crashes against the land, waves pick up pebbles and sand and hurl them against the coast. This makes parts of the coast break off. In some places, the rock is soft and is worn away, leaving a wide curve in the land called a bay. In other places, where the rock is hard, a finger of land stands out from the coast. This is called a headland.

stack

bay

arch

3 When the top of the rock arch falls into the sea, a tall pillar of rock is left behind. This is called a stack.

headland

2 The caves grow larger and may eventually meet in the middle, leaving an arch of rock.

cliff

cave

1 At the bottom of a headland, waves eat into the rock, making a cave. Sometimes, waves make caves on both sides of a headland.

Erosion by ice

A **glacier** is a slow-moving river of ice which usually forms high in the mountains. As a glacier slides down a mountain, the ice picks up rocks. These rocks scratch and scrape away the side of the mountain, making a deep **valley**.

snout
The end of a glacier is called the snout. .

melting ice
Rocks are carried away by melting ice. ....

Wind erosion

In deserts, there are few plants to protect the land from the wind, so soft rock is slowly worn away. The wind also flings grains of sand at hard rocks, smoothing the edges, like sandpaper. Over years, the wind carves rocks into strange shapes, as this picture of a rock in Colorado, in the USA, shows.

Protecting soil

Usually, erosion happens slowly over a long period of time, but it can be speeded up by storms, or when trees and plants are cut down. Then, the soil may blow away, or be washed downhill. People cut steps, called terraces, into the sides of mountains, to stop soil sliding down mountainsides. In the Philippines, farmers grow rice on the terraces.

Go to Animal life page 34, Mountain page 30, Volcano page 12, Where on Earth? page 42

Ocean

The ocean is a huge area of **salt water** that covers most of the Earth's surface. It is split into five main parts: the Pacific, Atlantic, Indian, Southern and Arctic oceans. Some oceans have smaller parts called seas. The water in the oceans is always moving. At the surface, the wind whips the water into waves that crash on to the land. Deep down, warm and cold rivers of water, called **currents**, flow through the oceans of the world.

▶ The average depth of the ocean is 4,000m. On the ocean floor, there are mountains, deep **valleys** and huge, flat plains, just as there are on dry land.

seamount
Under the water, there are **volcanoes** called seamounts. Waves may wear away the top of a seamount to leave a flat top.

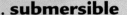

submersible
Underwater machines, called submersibles, help people to explore life on the ocean floor.

ocean ridge
A long row of mountains runs along the middle of each ocean. This is called an ocean ridge.

▼ Life in the ocean

Seaweed floats on the ocean surface and clings to rocks on the shore. Fish eat seaweed and also use it as a hiding place.

Water near the top of the ocean is warm and sunny. Tiny animals and plants, called plankton, live here. Many sea creatures depend on plankton for food.

Shoals of mackerel and other fish live about 200m below the surface. Mackerel are powerful swimmers that zoom through water looking for food.

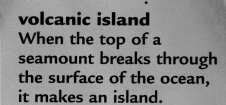

volcanic island
When the top of a seamount breaks through the surface of the ocean, it makes an island.

continental shelf
From the edge of a **continent**, the land slopes gently downwards and outwards under the ocean.

trench
A trench is a long, deep valley on the ocean floor. No one knows what lives at the bottom.

continental slope
At the end of the continental shelf, the land plunges down to the deep ocean floor.

Factfile

The world's longest mountain range, the Mid-Atlantic Ridge, runs down the middle of the Atlantic Ocean.

The Pacific Ocean is bigger than all the land on Earth put together. It is the largest of all the oceans.

The deepest place on Earth is the Mariana Trench in the Pacific Ocean. It plunges down for 11,000m.

Sperm whales dive down as deep as 3,000m to catch squid and fish. They can hold their breath for almost two hours while they search for food.

On the dark ocean floor, tripod fish wait for a meal to swim or drift past them. These fish perch on their three extra-long fins.

Go to Animal life page 34, Plant life page 32, Where on Earth? page 42

Desert

A desert is a dry place where it hardly ever rains. Some deserts are cold all the time, but most are hot during the day and bitterly cold at night. Many deserts are sandy, but others are covered in stones and bare rock. There is little water in deserts, so only a few plants and animals can live here. In some parts of the world, people have adapted to life in the desert.

Arizona Desert
The Arizona Desert in North America is dry and rocky. Giant tables of hard rock stand high above the desert sands. Cactus plants thrive because they need very little water to survive. Some birds shelter from the sun by building their homes in cactus plants.

yucca
A yucca plant stores water in its stiff, narrow, pointed leaves.

cactus
A cactus stores water in its thick, fleshy stem.

root system
Cactus roots spread out just below the surface and soak up rain and dew.

20

The Sahara Desert

The Sahara Desert, in Africa, is the biggest desert in the world. It covers an area almost as big as the USA. Most of the Sahara Desert is stony, but in sandy places, the wind blows the sand into big hills called **dunes**. When the wind blows really hard, the sand flies through the air in a sandstorm.

Sand dunes

The shape of a sand dune depends on the way the wind is blowing.

1 When the wind blows from one direction, curved dunes, called barchans, form.

wind direction

2 When the wind blows from all around, star-shaped dunes appear.

wind direction

People in deserts

There is not enough water to grow crops in deserts, but many people live here. They move their animals and belongings from place to place in search of water and plants. These men are crossing the Syrian Desert in the Middle East. They are wearing long, loose clothes to protect themselves from the heat of the sun.

Australian desert animals

Most of the **continent** of Australia is desert. Lizards, such as the thorny devil, live here because they can survive higher temperatures than birds or **mammals**. Some animals sleep through the day, to avoid the sun. Other animals sleep through the hottest months of the year.

Go to Animal life page 34, Erosion page 16, Mountain page 30, Where on Earth? page 42

Polar lands

The polar lands are the places at the top and bottom of the Earth, around the North and South poles. The land around the North Pole is called the Arctic and the land around the South Pole is called the Antarctic. Both poles are always covered with ice and snow, making them the coldest places on Earth. Winters at the poles are long and dark, and summers are short and light.

Antarctica

Antarctica is a frozen **continent**. Most of the land is covered by a massive sheet of ice that stretches into the Southern Ocean. There are hardly any plants, but animals, such as penguins, live here and feed on fish.

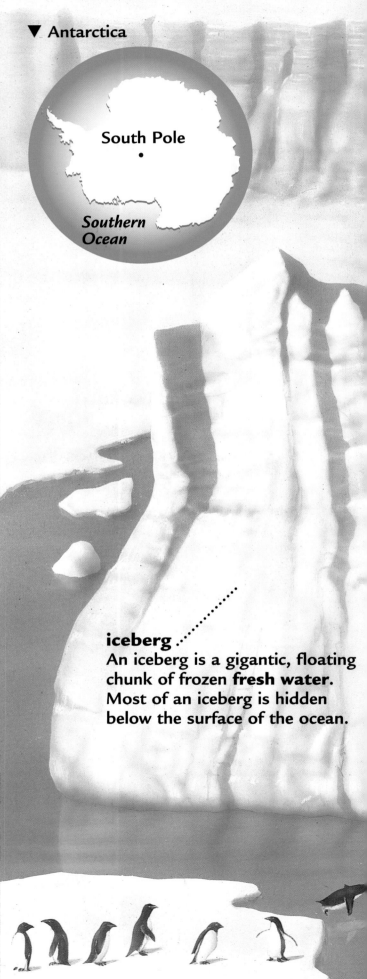

▼ Antarctica

South Pole

Southern Ocean

The Arctic

The Arctic is a frozen ocean surrounded by low land, called **tundra**, where no trees grow. Just below the surface of the tundra, the soil is always frozen. In winter, the ice in the Arctic Ocean spreads and meets the snowy tundra. In summer, a lot of the snow and ice melts. Then, for a short time, the tundra springs to life and small, colourful plants grow.

▼ The Arctic

Key

tundra

ice

North Pole

Arctic Ocean

iceberg
An iceberg is a gigantic, floating chunk of frozen **fresh water**. Most of an iceberg is hidden below the surface of the ocean.

glacier
An icy **glacier** creeps along the land. When it reaches the ocean, the end breaks off and an iceberg floats away.

People at the poles
Even though the poles are the coldest places on Earth, some people live and work here. These scientists are testing the temperature and saltiness of the water.

ice floe
Jagged sheets of ice, called floes, float on top of the ocean.

ice-breaker
An ice-breaker is a special ship that cuts a path through the ice, so that other ships can follow.

bergy bits
Often, small chunks of ice, called bergy bits, break off an iceberg.

pancake ice
In places, the ice turns slushy and forms round, soft pieces that look like pancakes.

Go to Animal life page 34, Plant life page 32, Where on Earth? page 42

Grasslands

Grasslands are vast areas of flat land with few trees, where little rain falls. There are two main types of grasslands. **Temperate** grasslands grow in cool places. They are called prairie in the USA, steppe in Asia and pampas in South America. Hot, **tropical** grasslands are known as savanna.

African savanna

Huge herds of animals wander this grassland, nibbling the grasses and leaves. After the rains, there is plenty of grass. Some animals eat the tops of the long grasses. Other animals eat the new shoots and seeds close to the ground.

giraffe
A giraffe uses its long tongue and curled top lip to strip leaves from high branches.

zebra
Large herds of zebra roam the savanna, feeding on the tops of the grasses.

gerenuk gazelle
Gerenuk can reach leaves and shoots on prickly bushes and low trees.

weaver birds
These birds weave blades of grass into hanging nests.

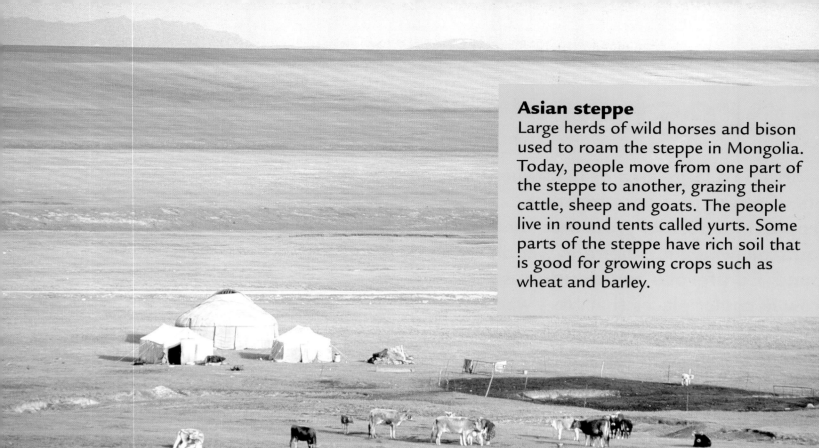

Asian steppe
Large herds of wild horses and bison used to roam the steppe in Mongolia. Today, people move from one part of the steppe to another, grazing their cattle, sheep and goats. The people live in round tents called yurts. Some parts of the steppe have rich soil that is good for growing crops such as wheat and barley.

North American prairie
The prairie is a huge area of land. In the past, millions of bison and antelope lived here, but today the land is ploughed and planted with wheat and corn to feed people. All the wheat is grown to the same height so that a machine can harvest it quickly.

South American pampas
The pampas does not get very hot, or very cold, which makes it the perfect place for growing corn and barley and for grazing animals. Thousands of sheep and cattle live on enormous ranches that stretch across the pampas. The cattle-farmers of Argentina are famous for rounding up the herds on horseback.

25

Go to Animal life page 34, Mountain page 30, Plant life page 32, Where on Earth? page 42

Forest

A forest is a large area of land where lots of trees grow close together. **Tropical** rainforests grow near the **Equator**, where it is hot and wet all year round. **Coniferous** and **deciduous** forests grow in cooler places that have warm summers and cool winters. Forests are home to people and all kinds of wildlife.

Coniferous forests

Trees that grow in coniferous forests have waxy, green needle-like leaves that stay on the branches all year round. Conifer seeds grow in woody cones. Most of the wood that is used to build homes and to make paper comes from conifers such as pine and spruce.

Deciduous forests

Deciduous trees, such as oak and beech, usually have wide, flat leaves. In summer, the leaves are green, but in autumn, they turn red, then golden-brown. Finally, the leaves die and fall to the ground. In winter, the branches are bare, but in spring they come back to life and new leaves grow.

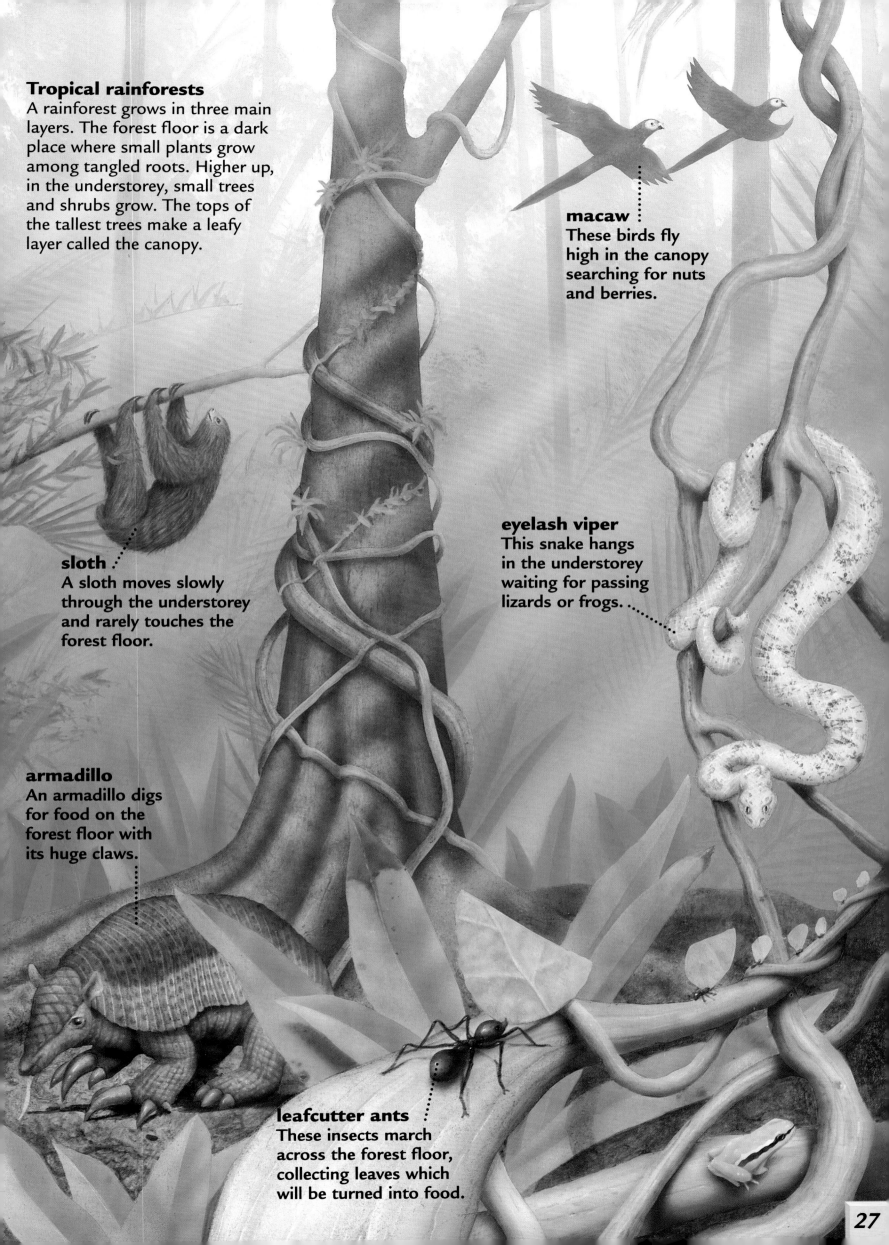

Tropical rainforests
A rainforest grows in three main layers. The forest floor is a dark place where small plants grow among tangled roots. Higher up, in the understorey, small trees and shrubs grow. The tops of the tallest trees make a leafy layer called the canopy.

macaw
These birds fly high in the canopy searching for nuts and berries.

sloth
A sloth moves slowly through the understorey and rarely touches the forest floor.

eyelash viper
This snake hangs in the understorey waiting for passing lizards or frogs.

armadillo
An armadillo digs for food on the forest floor with its huge claws.

leafcutter ants
These insects march across the forest floor, collecting leaves which will be turned into food.

27

Go to Erosion page 16, Mountain page 30, Where on Earth? page 42

River

A river is a large stream of **fresh water** that flows into another river, a lake, or the ocean. The water comes from rain or snow, or even from underground. A river usually begins high in the mountains, then races downhill. As a river moves along, it changes the shape of the land, cutting into rock and breaking up the soil.

▶ A river flows quickly through the mountains, but as more water flows into it, the river grows bigger and moves more slowly on its way to the ocean.

meander
A river twists and turns in huge loops, called meanders, across flat land.

source
The start of a river is called the source. A lake is the source of this river.

valley
As a river flows down a mountain, it carves out a deep **valley** in the land.

waterfall
Sometimes, a river plunges over a step of hard rock, carving into soft rock below. This is called a waterfall.

▼ How people use rivers

On a mountain, a fast-flowing river can be used to turn a water wheel. As the wheel turns, it moves machinery that grinds grain into flour.

A dam is a huge wall built in the mountains to hold back river water. Water flowing inside a dam can drive machines that make electricity.

Further down the river, the water is calmer. Here, people use the river to travel from place to place, and to go fishing and sailing.

Underground rivers

Most rivers flow above ground, but some flow below ground. Certain kinds of rocks allow water to pass through them. Then, a river seeps down through the rocks and runs along underground. The river eats into rocks and carves out caves. Some caves are as big as several football pitches. These are called caverns.

mouth of a river

The end of a river is called the mouth. When a river flows into the ocean, the fresh river water mixes with the **salt water**.

town

Often, towns grow up near rivers. Towns take their drinking water from the river..

delta

At the mouth of a river, piles of mud and sand collect in a fan shape. This is called a delta.

In places where the river is wide and slow-moving, people move heavy goods from one town, or factory, to another by boat.

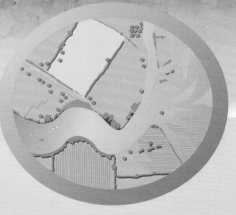

Towards the end of a river, the water often floods the land, spreading rich mud over the soil. This land is good for farming and growing crops.

Factfile

The Nile River, in Africa, is 6,671km long. It is the world's longest river.

Together, the Brahmaputra and Ganges rivers in India form the largest delta in the world.

The Colorado River, in the USA, has cut a valley so deep that it takes a day to walk from the top to the bottom.

Go to Continent page 8, Erosion page 16, Forest page 26, River page 28, Volcano page 12, Where on Earth? page 42

Mountain

A mountain is a part of the Earth's surface that rises up steeply from the surrounding land. Mountains are much larger than hills and take millions of years to form. Often, mountains are grouped together in long lines called chains. Some mountain chains are gradually growing taller, while others are being worn away.

mountain ridge
An icy **glacier** can tear away rock on a mountain top. When it melts, a sharp, narrow ridge is left behind.

jagged peaks
Freezing weather makes mountain rocks split to form rough, jagged peaks.

Changing mountains
As soon as mountains form, rain, wind, snow and ice start to eat into them. The softer rocks are worn away, leaving big dips called **valleys**. Harder rocks stand out as peaks. Young mountains usually have high, jagged tops. Old mountains are lower and more rounded because they have been worn away.

river valleys
Rivers cut down into mountain slopes, carving valleys with steep sides.

▼ How mountains form

Fold mountains
When two of the Earth's **plates** crash into each other, the rocks in the middle are pushed up to make fold mountains.

Volcanic mountains
When **magma** pours on to the Earth's surface, it cools and hardens. Over many years, it can form **volcanic** mountains.

Block mountains
Sometimes, blocks of rock split and slide along **fault lines**. One block may be lifted above another to form block mountains.

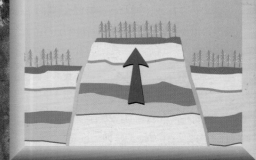

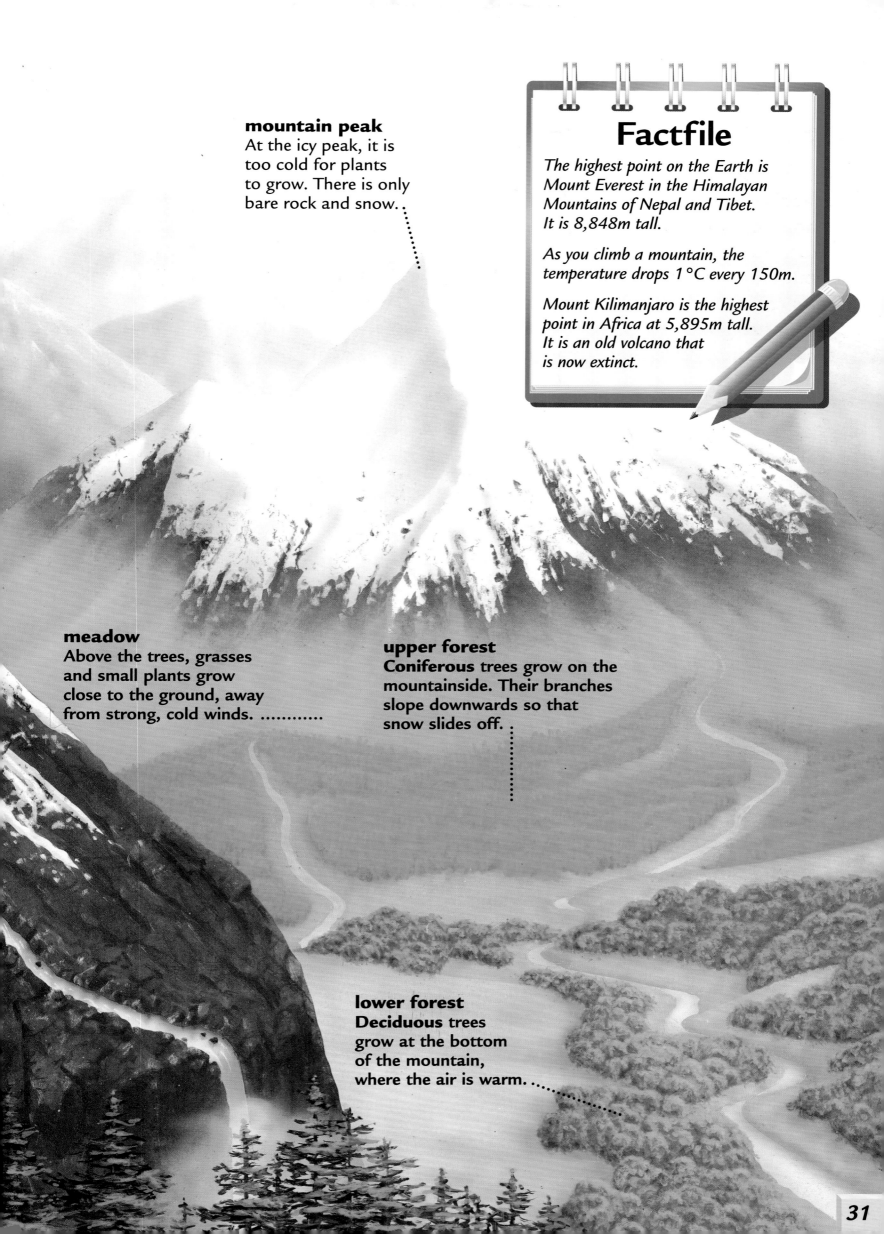

mountain peak
At the icy peak, it is too cold for plants to grow. There is only bare rock and snow. .

Factfile

The highest point on the Earth is Mount Everest in the Himalayan Mountains of Nepal and Tibet. It is 8,848m tall.

As you climb a mountain, the temperature drops 1°C every 150m.

Mount Kilimanjaro is the highest point in Africa at 5,895m tall. It is an old volcano that is now extinct.

meadow
Above the trees, grasses and small plants grow close to the ground, away from strong, cold winds. ....

upper forest
Coniferous trees grow on the mountainside. Their branches slope downwards so that snow slides off. .

lower forest
Deciduous trees grow at the bottom of the mountain, where the air is warm. ....

Go to Forest page 26, The Earth and its future page 40

Plant life

Plants are living things that grow all over the Earth. Unlike animals, plants do not move around to find food. Instead, they are fixed in one place and they make their own food. Most plants, from tall trees to short grasses, have flowers. The flower is the part of the plant that makes seeds, from which new plants grow. Other plants, including ferns and mosses, do not have flowers or seeds.

▼ There are more than 260,000 different kinds of plants, from towering trees to spiky grasses, pretty flowers, leafy ferns and creeping mosses.

How a plant makes food

A plant takes a **gas** called carbon dioxide from the air and soaks up water from the soil. Leaves trap the Sun's energy and use it to turn the water and carbon dioxide into food that helps the plant to grow.

sunlight

leaves take in carbon dioxide ....

roots take in water ....

flowers
Inside each flower, there is a dust called pollen. Bees and other insects carry the pollen from one flower to another, helping new seeds to grow.

liverworts

mosses

liverworts and mosses
These small plants live in shady, moist places. They cling to surfaces with many tiny hair-like strands.

▼ How plants scatter seeds

Blackberry seeds grow inside a fruit. Birds eat the fruit and the seeds pass out in their droppings.

Dandelion seeds float through the air like fluffy parachutes.

Seeds of the sycamore tree grow inside pods. When a pod splits open, the seeds fly far and wide.

trees
Trees are the largest and longest-living plants on Earth. Many of them grow fruit that is good to eat.

grasses
Grasses are one of the largest groups of plants. All grasses grow tiny flowers.

ferns
Ferns are one of the oldest groups of plants on Earth. They are anchored in the soil by roots that soak up water.

algae
This green film looks like a plant, but it is made of living creatures called algae.

Go to Desert page 20, Forest page 26, Grasslands page 24, Ocean page 18

Animal life

The Earth is a special **planet**. The **climate**, temperature and plant life have created the right conditions for animals to live on land, in the air and in the ocean. Scientists have divided animals into groups to make it easy to study them. **Mammals, reptiles,** birds, fish and amphibians all have backbones and scientists call them **vertebrates**. A large group of animals, which includes insects, does not have backbones. These animals are called **invertebrates**.

Birds
Birds are the only animals that have feathers and almost all birds can fly. A baby bird hatches from an egg that has a hard, waterproof shell. After a few weeks, the bird's feathers develop and its wings grow strong. Adult birds, such as this bald eagle, spend most of their days flying in the sky.

Mammals
Mammals are the only animals that have fur or hair. A female mammal, such as this lioness, gives birth to live young. She feeds her babies on milk which she makes in her body. There are mammals that live on land, underground, in water, and even some that can fly. People are mammals, too.

Reptiles

Crocodiles, snakes and lizards belong to a group of animals called reptiles. Most reptiles live in hot places. Their skin is made of tough, overlapping scales that help to keep their bodies moist. Some reptiles lay eggs, while others give birth to live young. Like all reptiles, a baby crocodile looks exactly like its parents, except that it is much smaller.

Amphibians

Frogs, toads, newts and salamanders belong to a group of animals called amphibians. Like all amphibians, this frog lives both in and out of the water. On land, a frog stays in damp places because it needs to keep its skin moist. Amphibian babies hatch from eggs laid in water or on damp ground.

Insects

There are more insects on the Earth than any other kind of animal. An adult insect has six legs and its body is made up of three parts. Most insects also have two feelers, called antennae, which they use for feeling and smelling. Many insects can fly. This beetle has a hard, red wing case to protect its wings.

Fish

Fish come in many shapes, sizes and colours. They can live in near-freezing oceans or warm **tropical** seas. Like most fish, this angelfish has fins for swimming and skin made of slippery scales. A fish breathes underwater. It has openings on each side of its head, called gills, which take in a **gas**, called oxygen, from the water.

Go to Climate and season page 38, The Earth and its future page 40

Weather

Sunshine, rain, wind and snow are all different kinds of **weather**. The weather that happens on Earth every day is caused by the Sun's rays heating the air around the Earth. As the air is warmed, it moves, carrying heat and water around the world. The amount of heat and water in the air makes the weather change from place to place.

Rainbows
Rainbows happen when the sun shines through the rain. The raindrops split the sunlight into all its colours. There are seven main colours in a rainbow and they are always in the same order – red, orange, yellow, green, blue, indigo and violet.

The water cycle
There is water everywhere on Earth – in rivers, in oceans and even in the air. Water moves from the oceans and land, to the air, to the land and back to the oceans again. This is called the **water cycle**.

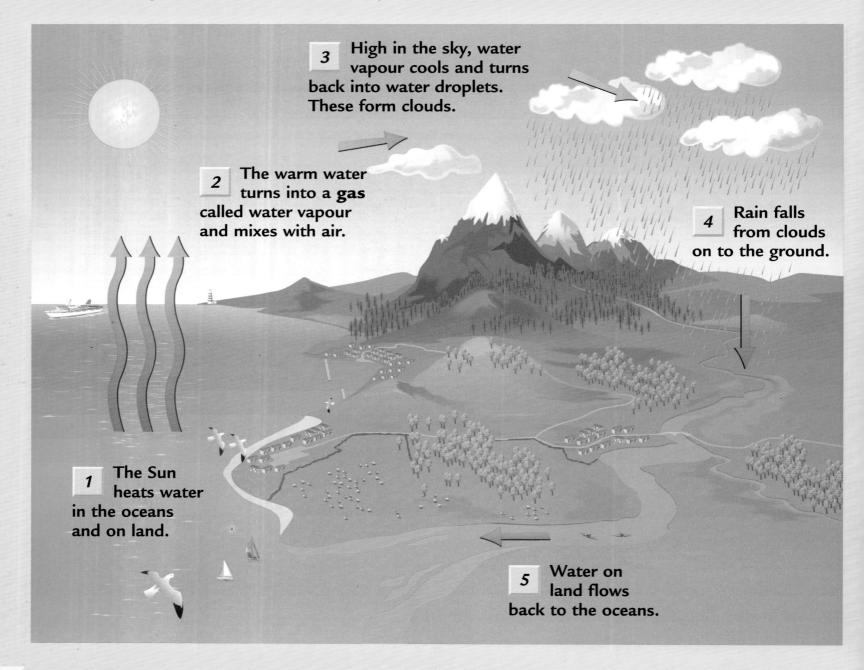

3 High in the sky, water vapour cools and turns back into water droplets. These form clouds.

2 The warm water turns into a **gas** called water vapour and mixes with air.

4 Rain falls from clouds on to the ground.

1 The Sun heats water in the oceans and on land.

5 Water on land flows back to the oceans.

Types of cloud
There are three main cloud shapes that can help you to tell what kind of weather may happen.

Cirrus clouds
Thin and wispy clouds show that the weather is changing.

Cumulus clouds
Fluffy clouds that look like cotton wool spell fair weather.

Stratus clouds
Long, flat clouds low in the sky show that rain is on the way.

Wind
The wind may blow gently as a breeze, or so hard that it pushes over trees. Wind is moving air. It happens because the Sun heats the land, which warms the air above it. In hot places, warm air rises. Then, cool air from colder places rushes in to take the place of the warm air. We feel this moving air as wind.

Electrical storms
Bad weather can bring storms with black clouds, strong winds, heavy rain and even thunder and lightning. A flash of lightning is a huge spark of electricity that jumps across the sky. Lightning heats up the air around it quickly, shaking the air and making the sound we call thunder.

Go to Animal life page 34, Weather page 36

Climate and season

Climate is a pattern of **weather** that is roughly the same from one year to the next. Some places have warm climates while others have cold climates. The climate of a particular place depends mostly on where it is in the world. In many places, the weather changes throughout the year. These changes are called **seasons**.

World climates

Places near the **Equator** are hot and wet all year round. They have a **tropical** climate. At the poles, the climate is cold and dry. In between, the climate is usually **temperate**, which means that it is mild and damp.

Key

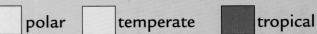

□ polar   □ temperate   ■ tropical

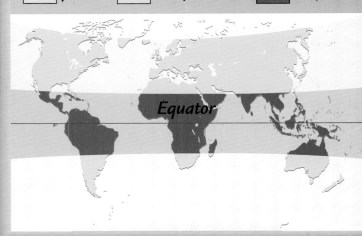

Equator

▼ This picture shows why some places on Earth have cold climates and others have hot climates.

The Sun warms all of the Earth, but shines more strongly on some parts of it than on others. This is because the Earth is curved.

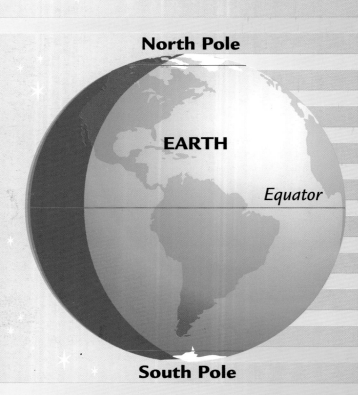

North Pole

EARTH

Equator

South Pole

SUN

At the Equator, the Sun's rays hit the Earth directly, making it very hot.

At the North and South poles, the Sun's rays are spread out and give less heat. Polar lands are very cold.

Four seasons

Temperate places have four seasons. In winter, days are short and cold. Spring days are longer and brighter. Summer days are warm and sunny. Cool weather returns in autumn.

Spring
On a cherry tree, small leaves and buds appear.

Summer
The tree keeps its leaves over the summer season.

Autumn
Leaves turn golden, then brown, die and drop off.

Winter
The bare tree stores its energy until spring.

Hibernation

Some animals change their habits with the seasons. During cold winter months, dormice, hedgehogs and marmots fall into a deep sleep called hibernation. They live off fat stored in their bodies. Hibernating animals wake up when spring arrives and days are warmer.

Wet and dry seasons

Some hot places near the Equator, such as India, have two main seasons in a year, one dry and one wet. These are called monsoon seasons. In the winter monsoon, hot, dry winds bake the land. During the summer monsoon, fierce winds bring clouds and lots of rain. Often there are floods in towns and cities.

Go to Forest page 26, Plant life page 32, Weather page 36

The Earth and its future

Many millions of people live on the Earth, and the way we live is changing the **planet**. People are cutting down forests and allowing poisonous **gases** to pollute the Earth's **atmosphere**. We need to repair the damage and look after the world's **natural resources** for the future.

Global warming
There is a layer of gas around the Earth which traps some of the Earth's heat. Fumes from cars, factories and burning forests mix with the gas layer and trap even more heat. Slowly, this is making the Earth warm up. This is called global warming. If the water in the oceans warms up too, then the level of the sea will rise and towns and cities on the coast may be flooded.

Acid rain
In some places, gases from cars and factories mix with water in the air. The gases turn to acid and become part of the **water cycle**, falling as **acid rain**. This can kill wildlife and destroy whole forests.

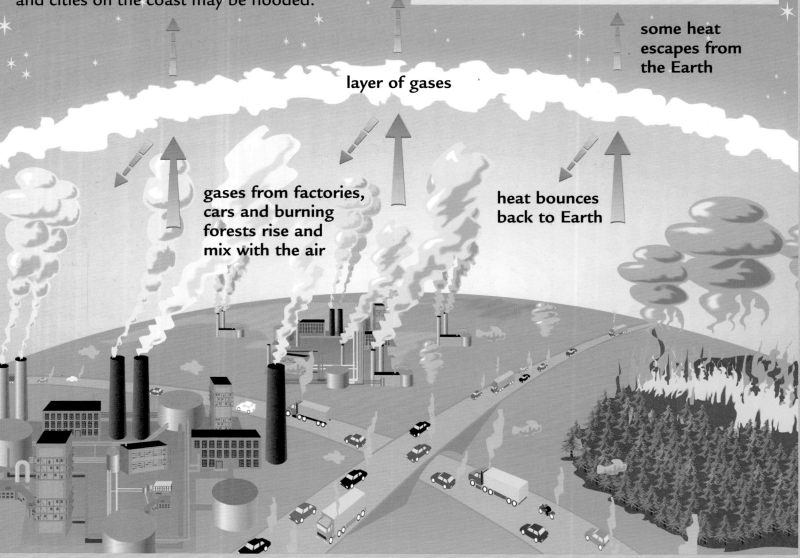

some heat escapes from the Earth

layer of gases

gases from factories, cars and burning forests rise and mix with the air

heat bounces back to Earth

Ozone holes

High above the Earth, there is a layer of gas called **ozone**. Ozone works like a shield, protecting people, animals and plants from the harmful rays of the Sun. Gases, called CFCs, from factories, refrigerators and aerosols destroy ozone. This picture was taken from space. The dark blue circle above Antarctica shows a growing hole in the ozone layer.

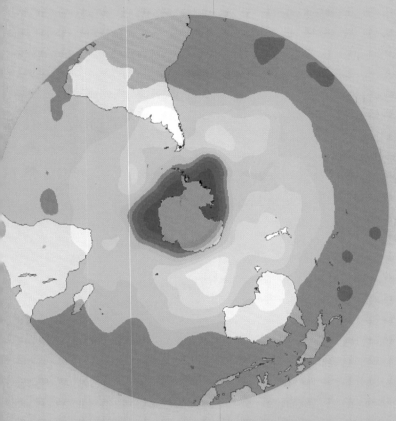

Wind power

We use **oil** and gas, which are natural resources, to make electricity. These fuels pollute the atmosphere, and one day they may also run out. Today, many countries make electricity using energy from the Sun, waves and wind. This energy is much cleaner and will not run out. These windmills use the wind to make enough electricity to supply thousands of homes.

Planting trees

Many people are working hard to protect the Earth and to look after its resources. The boy in this picture is growing trees from seeds to plant in the forest. Trees are important because they give off a gas called oxygen which all living things need to survive. Too many trees have been cut down in the past for wood, or to make space for farmland. Now, many more trees need to be planted for the future.

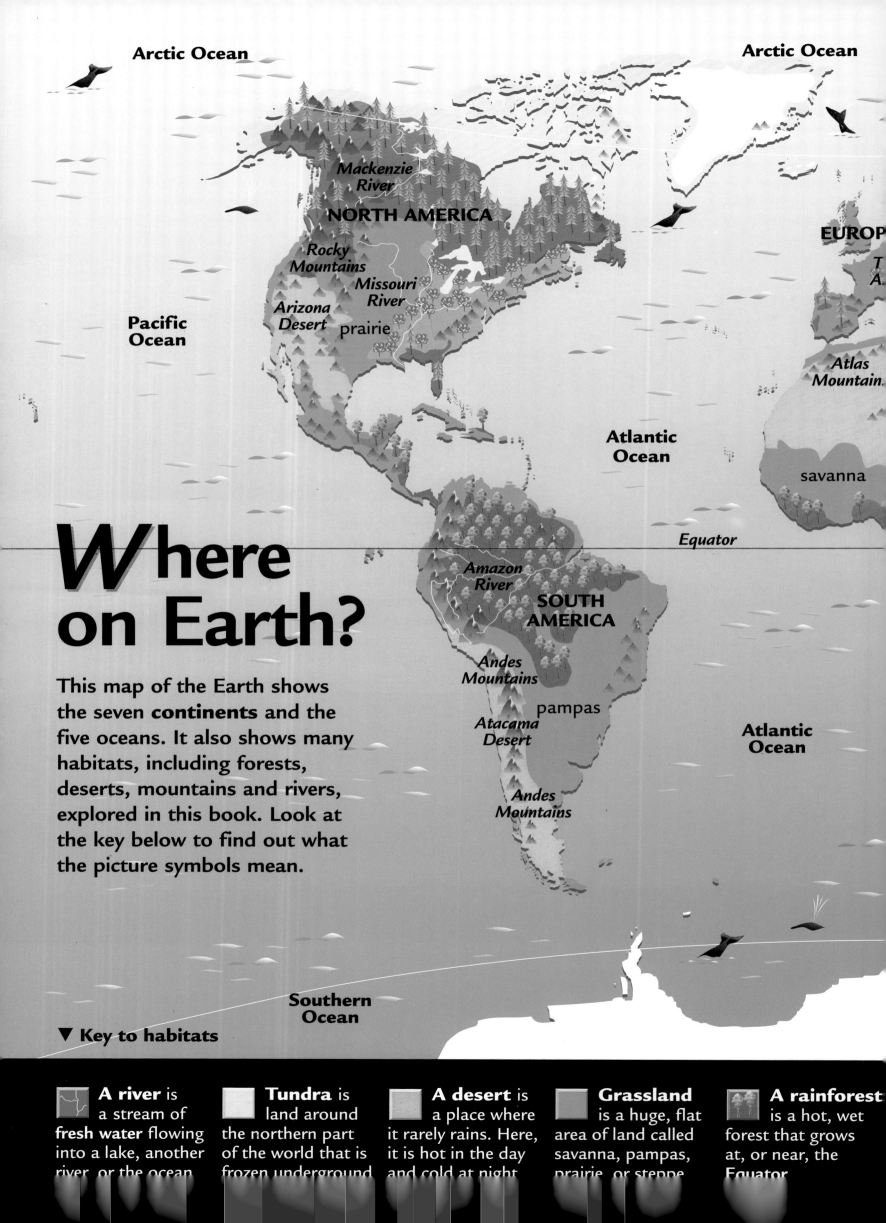

Arctic Ocean

Arctic Ocean

NORTH AMERICA

Mackenzie River

Rocky Mountains

Missouri River

Arizona Desert

prairie

EUROP

A

Atlas Mountain.

Pacific Ocean

Atlantic Ocean

savanna

Equator

Where on Earth?

This map of the Earth shows the seven **continents** and the five oceans. It also shows many habitats, including forests, deserts, mountains and rivers, explored in this book. Look at the key below to find out what the picture symbols mean.

Amazon River

SOUTH AMERICA

Andes Mountains

pampas

Atacama Desert

Atlantic Ocean

Andes Mountains

Southern Ocean

▼ Key to habitats

A river is a stream of **fresh water** flowing into a lake, another river, or the ocean.

Tundra is land around the northern part of the world that is frozen underground.

A desert is a place where it rarely rains. Here, it is hot in the day and cold at night.

Grassland is a huge, flat area of land called savanna, pampas, prairie, or steppe.

A rainforest is a hot, wet forest that grows at, or near, the Equator.

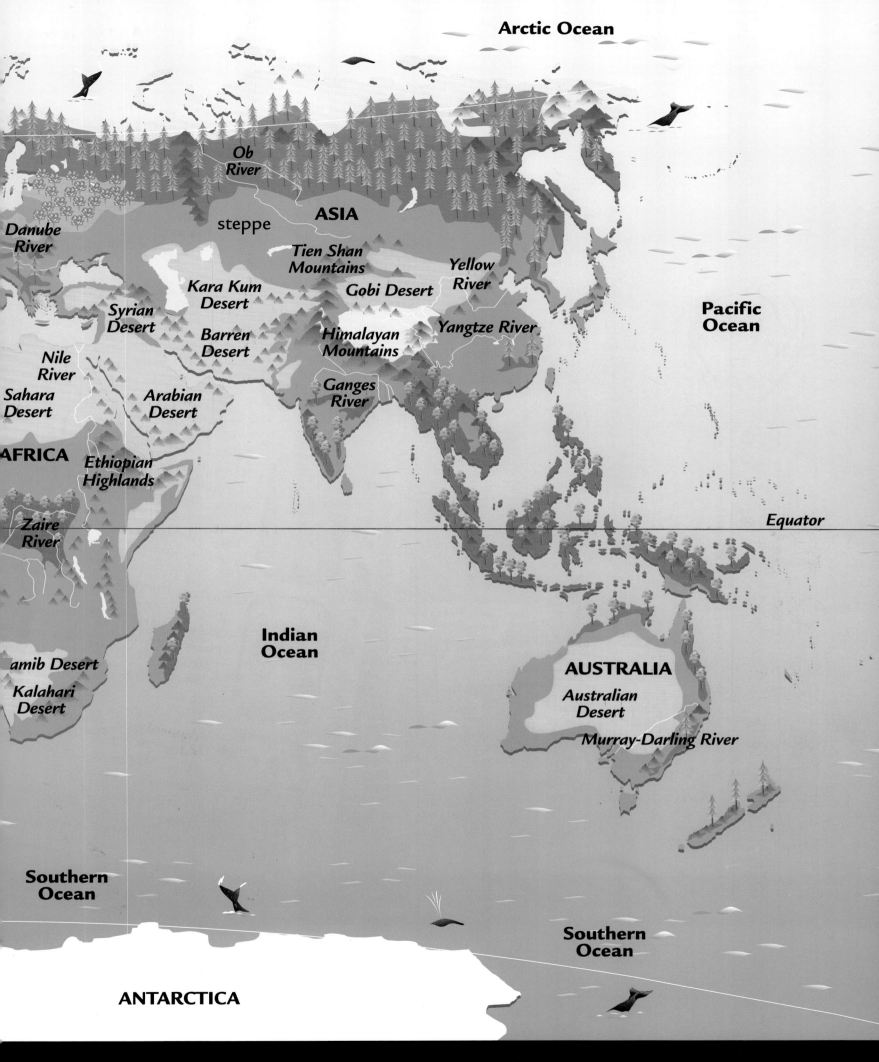

Arctic Ocean

Ob
River

ASIA

steppe

Tien Shan
Mountains

Yellow
River

Kara Kum
Desert

Gobi Desert

**Pacific
Ocean**

Syrian
Desert

Barren
Desert

Himalayan
Mountains

Yangtze River

Nile
River

Arabian
Desert

Ganges
River

Sahara
Desert

AFRICA

Ethiopian
Highlands

Zaire
River

Equator

**Indian
Ocean**

amib Desert

Kalahari
Desert

AUSTRALIA

Australian
Desert

Murray-Darling River

Danube
River

**Southern
Ocean**

**Southern
Ocean**

ANTARCTICA

**A deciduous
forest** is a forest
of trees that lose their
leaves in autumn and
grow new ones in spring

**A coniferous
forest** is a forest
of trees that keep their
leaves and stay green
all year round

**A mountain
chain** is a long
line of mountains that
are grouped together,
roughly side by side

Polar lands are
icy places at the
top and bottom of
the world, around the
North and South poles

Amazing facts

On these pages, you will discover amazing facts about the history of the Earth and about some of the **planet's** most unusual features. You will learn how many people live on Earth, and what may happen to it in the future.

Journey to the centre of the Earth

The centre of the Earth is 6,378km away. Starting at the crust, if you walked non-stop, you would reach the centre of the Earth in about 128 days. If you break the journey down, it would take you...

EARTH

centre

core

mantle

crust

> ...half a day to walk through the crust.

> ...58 days to walk through the mantle.

> ...70 days to walk through the core to the centre.

Earth file

Highest waterfall
Name: Angel Falls
Place: Venezuela, South America
Fact: The water drops a total of 979m.

Saltiest Sea
Name: Dead Sea
Place: Southwest Asia
Fact: This sea is so salty that it is impossible for people to sink.

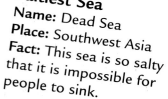

Tallest sand dunes
Name: Isaouane-N-Tifernine
Place: Algeria, North Africa
Fact: The highest dunes reach 465m.

Fastest moving glacier
Name: Quarauac Glacier
Place: Greenland
Fact: The glacier slides downhill, up to 24m in a day.

Most active volcano
Name: Stromboli
Place: Mediterranean Sea
Fact: When the volcano is active, it erupts continually for months, or even years at a time.

Earth timeline

The Earth formed about 4.5 **billion** years ago, but this is so long ago that it is difficult to imagine. It is easier to think of short lengths of time, such as hours or days. Imagine that the Earth began 24 hours ago, at midnight. These clocks tell you when everything else formed.

12 midnight

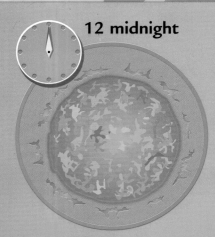

At **12.00 midnight,** the Earth began. At first it was a fiery, hot ball.

6.10 at night

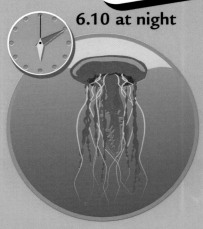

At **6.10,** over 18 hours later, jellyfish and other simple animals appeared.

9.50 at night

At **9.50,** the first fish, including sharks, swam in the oceans.

How many people?

Fifty years ago, about 2.5 billion people lived on the planet. Better medicines and more food meant that many people began to live longer.

Today, there are almost 6 billion people on Earth – more than double the number of 50 years ago. Many people live longer than ever before.

If the number of people on the Earth continues to grow at this rate, then 100 years from now, there will be an incredible 12 billion people on Earth.

50 years ago

today

100 years from now

Strange weather

When storms rage and the weather is dramatic, strange things can happen.

Terrible twister
In 1931, in the USA, a twisting wind, called a tornado, lifted an 83-tonne train into the air and dropped it in a ditch nearby.

Heavy hailstones
The heaviest hailstones ever recorded fell in Bangladesh in 1986. They weighed 1kg, about as much as a small melon.

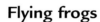

Flying frogs
A shower of frogs fell from the sky in England in 1954. Strong winds picked up the frogs from their watery homes and carried them through the air.

What will happen to the Earth in the future?

The world is slowly warming up. If the temperature of the Earth rises by 4°C, this could heat up the water in the oceans and make it rise. Cities such as New York could be flooded.

Thousands of years from now, the Earth may cool down. There could be a big ice age, which means that ice would cover much of the Earth's surface. The last ice age was 10,000 years ago.

10.15 at night

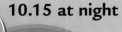

10.30 at night

10.45 at night

11.59.55 (secs) at night

At 10.15, giant insects and millepedes up to 2m long, crawled across the land.

At 10.30, the first trees started to grow. They were **coniferous** trees.

At 10.45, the first dinosaurs roamed the planet.

At 5 seconds to midnight, or just 5 seconds ago, people like us appeared.

Glossary

acid rain Rain that is more acid than usual because it is polluted by car and factory fumes.

atmosphere A layer of **gas** that surrounds the Earth. The Earth's atmosphere, which is called the air, is a mixture of different gases.

Big Bang A huge explosion, **billions** of years ago, which most scientists believe created the universe.

billion A number meaning one thousand million, written as 1,000,000,000.

climate The usual pattern of **weather** in a place over months or years.

coniferous Trees, such as pine and spruce, that have cones and long, thin needle-like leaves.

continent One of the seven large areas of land on Earth. The world's continents are Europe, Asia, Africa, North America, South America, Australia and Antarctica.

crust The thin, rocky 'skin' around the outside of the Earth.

currents Warm or cold rivers of water moving through the oceans of the world.

deciduous Trees that lose their leaves in winter.

dune A mound of loose sand grains pushed into a large pile by the wind.

Equator An imaginary line around the middle of the Earth.

erosion The gradual wearing down and carrying away of rocks and soil by wind, water, or ice.

fault line A crack in the Earth's **crust**.

fresh water Water that is not salty.

gas An invisible substance, such as carbon dioxide, that is neither a liquid, nor a solid.

glacier A huge, slow-moving river of ice.

invertebrate An animal without a backbone.

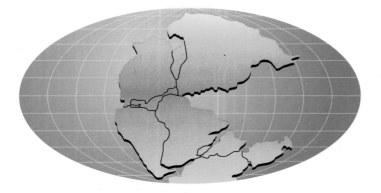

lava Hot, melted rock from inside the Earth that has spilled out on to the Earth's surface.

magma Hot, melted rock under the Earth's surface.

mammal A warm-blooded animal, with hair, that drinks its mother's milk when it is young.

mantle The thick layer of rock in the middle of the Earth, between the **crust** and the core. Rock that is close to the crust is melted, or molten.

natural resources Useful things that people take from the Earth, such as wood, plants, metals, **oil** and water.

oil A liquid made from the remains of plants and animals that lived in the ocean long ago. We burn oil for energy to power cars and machines.

ozone A type of **gas** in the Earth's **atmosphere** that shields the Earth from the Sun's harmful rays.

planet A large, round object in space, such as the Earth, that travels around the Sun or another star.

plate An enormous slab of rock that makes up part of the Earth's **crust** and sits under the oceans and **continents**.

reptile A cold-blooded animal with a dry, scaly skin, such as a snake or a crocodile, that breathes air. Some reptiles, though not all, lay eggs.

salt water Water in oceans, which tastes salty.

season A change in the **weather** that occurs at the same time each year.

temperate A **climate** with warm, rainy **weather** that is neither too hot nor too cold.

tropical Places near the **Equator** with hot **climates**. These places may have wet **weather** all year round, or have wet and dry **seasons**.

tundra Low, flat land around the Arctic, with frozen soil and no trees.

valley The lower land between hills or mountains.

vertebrate An animal with a backbone.

volcano An opening in the Earth's surface from which ash or hot, melted rock explodes.

water cycle The way that water travels from land and ocean, into the air, and falls to the Earth again.

weather All the rain, snow, wind and sunshine that happens when the air in the Earth's **atmosphere** warms up or cools down.

Index

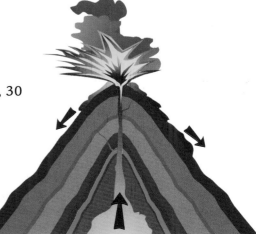